llege House, 45, East Street, Faversham, Kent. Faversham 2302. August 5th 1980.

TEN LITTLE BAD BOYS

KESTREL BOOKS
Published by Penguin Books Ltd, Harmondsworth,
Middlesex, England

Copyright © 1978 by Rodney Peppé

All rights reserved. No part of this publication may be reproduced, stored in a retrieval system, or transmitted in any form or by any means, electronic, mechanical, photocopying, recording or otherwise, without the prior permission of the Copyright owner.

First published in 1978

ISBN 0 7226 5431 6

Printed in Great Britain by Sackville Press Billericay Ltd

Other picture books by Rodney Peppé

THE ALPHABET BOOK
CIRCUS NUMBERS
THE HOUSE THAT JACK BUILT
HEY RIDDLE DIDDLE!
SIMPLE SIMON
CAT AND MOUSE
ODD ONE OUT
HUMPTY DUMPTY
PICTURE STORIES
RODNEY PEPPÉ'S PUZZLE BOOK

TEN LITTLE BAD BOYS

Rodney Peppé

Kestrel Books

Ten little bad boys went out to dine;

One choked his little self,

and then there were nine.

Nine little bad boys sat up very late;

One overslept himself,

and then there were eight.

Eight little bad boys travelling in Devon;

Seven little bad boys chopping up sticks;

One chopped himself in half,

and then there were six.

Six little bad boys playing with a hive;

A bumble-bee stung one,

and then there were five.

Five little bad boys going in for law;

One got in chancery,

and then there were four.

Four little bad boys going out to sea;

A red herring swallowed one,

HELP!

and then there were three.

Three little bad boys walking in the Zoo;

A big bear hugged one,

and then there were two.

Two little bad boys sitting in the sun;

One got frizzled up,

and then there was one.

One little bad boy living all alone;

He got married,

and then there were none.